The Royal Castle of

NEUSCHWANSTEIN

Description of the Castle · History of the Construction · The Sagas

Julius Desing

Photographys by Klaus und Wilhelm Kienberger

Verlag Wilhelm Kienberger Lechbruck

DOVICUS II.
AVARIAE REX.
CCCLXV.

The history of the construction of Neuschwanstein Castle

Building has always been a special privilege of kings and princely sovereigns, the royal family of Bavaria being no exception. It was not only King Ludwig II who develeped a veritable passion for building. Prince Max Emanuel, for example, had begun with the construction of a spacious castle, similar to the one at Versailles, in Schleissheim near Munich. This castle as well as two of Ludwig II's castles were never completed. Ludwig's father, Max II, had planned to relocate his entire court to a castle which was to be newly built in Feldafing, near Lake Starnberg. He also acquired the ruin of the old Schwanstein Castle in Allgaeu, in the southern part of Bavaria. He had this castle rebuilt and thus Hohenschwangau Castle became the family's summer residence. He also considered having the two old castle ruins, Vorderhohenschwangau and Hinterhohenschwangau rebuilt. However, he never carried out this plan.

Hohenschwangau Castle became the favorite residence of Ludwig II, the young king of Bavaria, after the death of his father in 1864. He praised "this paradise on earth, where I can live out my ideals and thus find happiness." Hohenschwangau was the source of inspiration from which this young sovereign later drew his ideas and, using the most modern methods and technical possibilities of the time, realized them in his own castles.

A visit to Wartburg Castle in Eisenach in May 1867, inspired Ludwig to build a romantic castle of his own. The following facts also must be considered: Bavaria was in a state of great need after having lost a war in 1866. How seriously Ludwig took this situation can be gathered from a newspaper article in the "Fuessener Blatt" from January 16, 1867: "Munich January 1: The royal court gardener, Mr. Effner, has been instructed to see to it immediately that work on various gardens is carried out as well as other types of jobs in order to reduce the prevailing unemployment as much as possible." This situation is likely to have further supported the King in taking up his father's old idea of having a second castle built in Hohenschwangau.

The site of the new castle has the following historical background: There were originally four castles in the town of Hohenschwangau, which in medieval times was a place of great strategic importance. One of these was Schwanstein which today is the castle of Hohenschwangau. Directly to the west of this castle, there was Castle Frauenstein, which today is only marked by a stone. The other two castles were located in the wooded hills southeast of the town of Hohenschwangau, the so-called "Neudeck".

The King had several drafts made for the castle (figures 3 and 4). The draft made by Christian Jank, a painter for the theater from Munich (figure 5), found, to a great extent, the King's approval.

2. Ruins of the two castles, Vorderhohenschwangau and Hinterhohenschwangau before 1830.

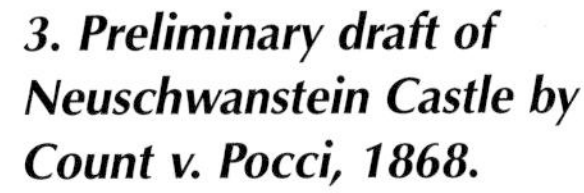

3. Preliminary draft of Neuschwanstein Castle by Count v. Pocci, 1868.

4. Draft of Neuschwanstein Castle by Christian Jank, 1868.

5. Draft of Neuschwanstein Castle by Christian Jank, 1869

The new castle did not require any special landscape gardening. Ludwig II was able to set his castle, like a precious stone in a beautiful mounting, into a magnificent natural cliff setting. Ludwig II placed great importance on creating harmony between the natural landscape and the building itself. All of his creations are proof that he was a master at doing just this.

The Royal Building Supervisor Riedel was trusted with planning the construction of the castle. It was under his direction that the building of the entire shell of the castle was carried out. In July 1868, after detailed study of the ground conditions, water pipes were laid and a road to the construction site was built. The ruins of the two old castles (figure 2) were pulled down and cleared away. Seven or eight meters (approx. 20 - 25 ft) at the top of the hill were blasted off in order to create a larger platform for construction. On September 5, 1869 the foundation stone for the "New Castle in Hohenschwangau" was laid and this giant building project could begin (figure 7).

After the foundation stone had been laid, almost all of the construction work was concentrated on the gate house (figure 8). Ludwig II, who had been impatiently watching the construction of the new castle from the Tassilo room of his father's castle of Hohenschwangau with a telescope, decided to have an apartment installed in the gate house so that he could directly observe the construction of his dream castle. Besides that it was possible to set up comfortable apartments for the building supervisors in this building. It was not until the gate house was finished and furnished in 1873 that the construction of the castle itself began (figure 9).

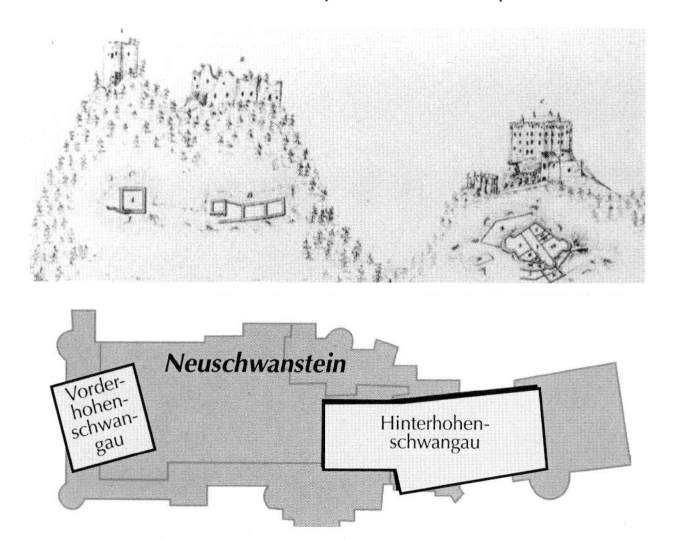

6. Sketches showing the position of the two castle ruins.

7. Laying the foundation stone for Neuschwanstein Castle in 1869.

8. Draft of the gate house, Christian Jank, 1869

At the same time that the construction on the castle began, a canteen for the some 200 workers was built below the construction site. This canteen soon became a popular place for excursions for the local population as well as for the many curious visitors who came in increasing numbers to Hohenschwangau. This canteen still exists and is now the well-known and modernized restaurant "Zur Neuen Burg".

Construction of the castle demanded an enormous amount of material. Alone in 1872, 450 tons (9000 hundredweight) of cement and 1,845 hectoliters of lime were used. Statistics covering the years 1879/80 list the following amount of material needed for construction:

465 tons of Salzburg marble
4550 tons of sandstone from Nuerting
400,000 bricks
3600 cubic meters of sand
600 tons of cement
50 tons of hard coal
2050 cubic meters of wooden scaffolding

9. The gate house, 1873

These figures give a clear indication of the economic importance of the King's construction plans, not only for the immediate area but also for all of Bavaria.
The huge amount of building material was transported up the newly built road on the west side of the main castle where it was pulled further up by a steam driven building crane. The building components were then brought to their next destination by dumping cars. From there the workers hoisted the parts further up with the help of various sized pulleys to the actual site where the parts would be finally used in the building process. Even in those days, the construction equipment was tested annually to ensure that it was in full working order and was operationally safe. This was carried out by an organization called the "Bayerischer Dampf-Kessel-Revisions-Verein" ("The Bavarian Steam-Boiler Monitoring Union") which today is known as the "TUV" and is responsible for technical check-ups.

There was also a revolutionary modern social system which was certainly unique at that time in all of Bavaria. On April 3, 1870 "The Union of Craftsmen for Construction of the Royal Castle of Hohenschwangau" came into being. It still exists today as the "Private Health Care Association" in Schwangau. The purpose of this association was to provide compensation of 65% of the wages (10.50 marks weekly) to injured or sick workers for a maximum of 15 weeks. The association was funded by the workers' payment of 70 pennies a week plus a considerable subsidy from the King. A plaque in the lower courtyard commemorates this social institution.

In 1872, Riedel, who up to that time had been the Royal Building Director, was replaced by Georg von Dollman who became chief architect and building director. The construction of the shell of the main castle took until January

10. State of construction in 1874

11. State of construction in 1875

12. Crane at the construction site of Neuschwanstein Castle

13. State of construction in 1880

14. State of construction in 1880

15. State of construction in 1880

1880. Finally, the enormous framework for the roof could be placed on the building. In 1881 the work on the interior of the 5th floor (Singers' Hall) and the 4th floor (the King's apartments) could begin.

Furnishing the rooms of the castle according to the King's wishes consumed a huge amount of money. Whereas until about 1881 costs were kept within the estimated range, the budget had to be greatly exceeded in order to stay within the time limit set by the King. Besides his other building projects, which had to be financed by Ludwig II himself as well, the building of Neuschwanstein during the last three years of the King's life amounted to 3.7 million marks compared with the 600,000 marks the King actually had planned on spending. The King consequently falling into debt by exceeding the building costs finally led to the so-called 'Tragedy of the King'. In order to get a rough idea of the building costs from a modern point of view it is necessary to compare wages and prices with those of today. A factory worker then earned about 100 marks a month, a bricklayer about 70 marks, a teacher about 120 marks and a higher government official about 500 marks. A pound of bread cost 10 pennies (pfennigs), a pound of meat 40 to 60 pennies and an egg 5 pennies. For a two-bedroom apartment in Munich one had to pay about 40 to 50 marks rent a month. From this one may reasonably conclude that one mark during the time when the castle was built would be equivalent to about 30 marks today.
All in all the cost of building Neuschwanstein amounted to 6,180,047 marks, all covered by the King's private funds, his royal appanage and funds belonging to the King's family. Ludwig II has been accused time and time again of ruining the Bavarian State through his building projects. There is, however, absolutely no basis for accusations of this kind. These accusations were put forth as a pretext of some sort to find an excuse for the treasonable measures taken against the King by the Lutz Administration.

Obviously, a building project of this nature took its toll of human lives. These also shall not be forgotten: On April 23, 1876 Herold, the site manager, shot himself at the building site, the motive for his suicide could never be clarified. On May 9, 1878 the carpenter Franz Straubinger fell from a two story high scaffolding and suffered fatal injuries. On February 25, 1880 the carpenter Moritz Mayr slipped while raising the timber for the roof and fell from this terrible height all the way down into the Poellat gorge. He was killed immediately. On July 20, 1882 the stonemason Klotz was found dead at the bottom of the gorge. The cause of his death has never been clarified. On June 25, 1883 Christian Woehrle, a stonemason, was killed by falling rocks at the quarry of Alterschrofen. (The limestone used to cover all the walls of the castle was taken from this quarry.)
More than hundred years later the castle took another victim: Herman Loderer, who had been working on covering the castle's roof for 18 years, fell from the roof down into the gorge on November 11, 1987 shortly before the work on the roof was completed. Again the cause of his death could never be fully explained.

16. State of construction in 1882

17. State of construction in 1885

18. State of construction in 1886

In 1884, Georg von Dollman, the building supervisor, was replaced by the architect Julius Hofmann, who also planned and carried out most of the interior decoration.

At the King's death on the 13th of June, 1886 Neuschwanstein was still only a construction site. As it was no longer possible to continue construction following the King's plans, the interior of the 3rd floor was never completed. It was here that a hall in the Moorish style as well as guest rooms were planned (figure 27).

In order to reach at least a partially intact architectural unity of the upper courtyard, the "Kemenate" (medieval living quarters for noble women) was completed according to the original plans by the architect Julius Hofmann. The building, however, was built without the decorative forms and the tower which were originally intended to be part of the castle (figure 23). The income from selling entrance tickets to the castle made it possible for the royal family to finance this construction. The massive keep (a heavily fortified main tower of a castle) with a height of 90 meters (approx. 270ft) along with the Gothic chapel on its first floor, which were intended to be the central building within the entire complex of Neuschwanstein, were never built (figures 19, 20, 21, 22, 24 and 25). The enormous high tower of the keep, together with the main castle, the "Kemenate", the "Ritterbau" (quarters for the knights) and the gate house would have constituted architectural unity as it was intended by the King.

When construction was stopped, the following buildings and rooms could no longer be completed for financial reasons:
The knights' bath which was to have been modeled on the one in Wartburg Castle. The king had planned to build the bath in the southwest part of the main castle directly under the Throne Hall where it would extend from the first to the second floor (figure 28). Today the entrance to the exit tunnel is located here. The boiler for the warm water had already been delivered in 1886 but it was never installed. From this bathing area there was to have been a door leading into a small park. Through the open doors visitors

19. Draft of the castle chapel, H. v. Pechmann, 1868

20. Draft of the castle chapel, Gg. Hauberrisser, 1870

21. Draft of the castle chapel, Peter Herwegen, 1870

22. Draft of the keep (medieval tower), E. Riedl, 1871

23. Construction of the "Kemenate"

24. Draft of the keep, Christian Jank, 1869

to the castle have a wonderful view of the old castle of Hohenschwangau and the surrounding lakes.
The bastion on the west side of the main castle with a fountain and gardens which one could have entered from the baths (figure 26).

The rooms on the third floor of the main castle which were to be modeled on the rooms of the Alhambra, residence of the Moorish kings, near Granada in Spain (figure 27).

The interior decoration of the "Kemenate". It wasn't until after World War II that the interior of the "Kemenate" was completed. Today there are offices for the administration and living quarters for the staff in this building (figure 23).

In summary it must be said that the construction of the castle was carried out according to a well thought-out plan. The castle was equipped with all kinds of technical conveniences which were very modern, if not to say revolutionary, at that time. For example:

Running water on all of the floors. As the spring which supplied the castle with excellent drinking water was located 200 meters (approx. 600 ft) above the castle, it was possible to supply the entire castle up to the top floor with water without the use of additional pumps. There were toilets equipped with automatic flushing on every floor.

A warm air central heating system for the entire building of the main castle.

A hot water system for the kitchen and for the bath, the bath, however, never going beyond the planning stage.

Two electrical interior staff locator systems with optical signals which ran on dry batteries. There was one for the valet on duty and one for the King's personal adjutant.

Two telephones on the fourth and fifth floors of the main castle.

25. Draft of the keep, Christian Jank, 1871

26. Draft of the bastion, H. Pruckner, 1885

28. Draft of the Knights' Hall, E. Riedl, 1870

27. Draft of the Moorish Hall on the 3rd floor

29. Bust of the King from 1988 (Foundry Braun, Oberschleissheim)

"Do not disturb the idyllic solitude of this romantic setting, whose picturesque beauty is even greater in winter than in summer, by building factories and railroads. For there will come a time when many other people will yearn, as I do, for such a piece of land where they can find refuge, a place left unspoiled by modern culture and technology, greed and haste, a place far from the noise and turmoil, the soot and dust of the cities."

(Ludwig II to Anton Memminger, planner of railroads)

The Red Corridor

The tour through Neuschwanstein Castle starts at the so-called "Red Corridor" on the second floor of the castle itself. This name goes back to the red tiles from Mettlach, which cover the floor passage.

It was the express wish of the King that there should be no portraits of himself within the castle. In 1988 the King Ludwig Club of Munich donated a bronze bust of the King, which is on exhibit here (figure 29). Thus every visitor has a chance to 'greet' the master of the house at the beginning of the tour.

When on June 12, 1986 the King was taken away from his favorite castle by a commission from Munich, he said to his servant Stich the following foreboding words: "Sticherl, keep up the rooms for me! Don't let them be profaned by curious spectators. I have spent the bitterest hours of my life here - I shall never return again!"

The servants' quarters were to be found on this floor. On the way to the main staircase one can have a look at a couple of the five servants' rooms through the open window. The rooms are still completely furnished. Each room was occupied by two servants. The furniture is made of oak (figure 32).

The walls along the corridor have small cast-iron doors close to the floor. These are the openings for the hot air central heating system, which during the King's lifetime was already capable of heating the entire castle. Except in the bedroom all the rooms in the King's living quarters had such heating vents. In the bedroom the warm air shutters were fitted unobtrusively into the wooden paneling.
The King's staircase which begins at the end of the "Red Corridor" was made of Untersberg marble, originating from Salzburg. Also the massive column in the center of the room is made of solid marble. The walls of the staircase are painted with stylized dragons. A painted frieze of deer and other game decorates the top of the middle column. It runs all the way up to the uppermost floor.

31. Entrance hall and the 'Red Corridor'

32. View of servants' rooms

The Entrance Hall to the Fourth Floor

Having passed the main staircase, which was exclusively reserved for the King's convenience whenever he resided in the castle (the servants used two smaller staircases), one reaches the entrance hall to the fourth floor of the castle (figure 33).

Behind the doors fitted with painted glass the first thing to catch one's eye is the magnificent ribbed vault. Painted coats of arms of Schwangau, Bavaria and Wittelbach carved from stone can be found at the intersections of the arches. Figures of animals sculptured from marble decorate the bases of the arches. Three large wrought iron chandeliers, set with candles and decorated with painted wrought iron swans, illuminated the hall. Two marble entrances lead to the King's quarters on the left and to the Throne Hall on the right. The wall paneling and the benches along the wall, some of which are richly decorated with woodcarvings, are made of oak. The entrance hall is of trapezoidal shape due to the huge monolith of dolomite that served as the foundation stone to the main castle. As the rock is rounded at this particular point it was necessary to give a trapezoidal shape to the entrance halls of all the floors. Thus those rooms intended as living quarters and as rooms of state could be designed in a rectangular form.

The windows are also well worth noting. The castle was built in the style of a medieval castle. However, in the 12th century glass window panes were unknown, so the King wished that windows without glass be feigned. Thus the window panes were fitted directly into the stone work of the arches as well as between the middle columns of the window frames. As a matter of fact, the windows at first glance actually do appear to have no window panes.

In Europe the first windows with glass were not in use before the 13th century. However, they were so expensive, that hardly anybody could afford them. In those days windows were covered with oil paper and wooden boards to keep the cold out. It was not until the beginning of the 15th century that glass was commonly used for windows.

Two oak doors, one next to the entrance to the main staircase and one next to the windows facing the gorge have magnificent wrought iron work. They lead to the smaller stairwells to be used by the servants.

33. Entrance hall, 4th floor

The walls of this entrance hall are decorated with numerous paintings which were painted onto a smooth layer of plaster-of-Paris to create an effect similar to fresco paintings. The Munich professor Wilhelm Hauschild illustrated scenes from the Sigurd saga as recorded in the "Edda", an earlier version of the Nibelungen song, which served as a model for Richard Wagner's "Ring of the Nibelung".

Here is an abridged version of the Sigurd saga:

The Asen, a group of Germanic Gods, had their castle Wallhall built by giants, whom they rewarded with an enormous treasure. This treasure, however, had been illegally obtained by Loki, the God of Fire, from Alberich, the master of the World of Fogs (Nibelungen - from the German 'Nebel' = fog). Alberich thereupon curses this "Nibelungen Treasure" - it is to bring great misfortune to any future owner. Because of this treasure Hreidmar, the old chief of the giants, is killed by his son Fafnir who then drives Regin, Hreidmar's second son, from their home. Fafnir changes into a dragon, who jealously guards the treasure. Regin, however, has never stopped wishing to possess this treasure. He settles down as a blacksmith near Fafnir's den. On one of his journeys young Sigurd meets his uncle Gripir at the court of Prince Geitir. Gripir foretells his nephew the fate awaiting him (figure 35).

34. Right: Sigurd's ride through burning flames: *"On the highlands sleeps the emperor's daughter, bright in her armor ..."* ***Left: Gudrun hands Sigurd the cup with the potion of oblivion.***

35. Gripir: *"Alone shalt thou kill the shimmering dragon..."*

36. Gudrun waits for Sigurd: *"What hast thou done with Sigurd, the noble hero,..."*

37. Brynhild mocks Gunnar: *"There laughed Brynhild, Budli's daughter, a laugh from the bottom of her heart..."*

On one of his many journeys Sigurd meets Regin who teaches him to become a blacksmith. Together they forge the magnificent sword "Gram" (figure 33).

Regin hands this invincible weapon to young Sigurd, whom he tells about Fafnir's incredible treasure. Sigurd kills the dragon and bathes himself in the blood streaming from its wounds (figure 38).
This bath in the dragon's blood renders his body invulnerable, except for one tiny spot on his back which was not covered with the dragon's blood. Bathing in the dragon's blood also has enabled Sigurd to suddenly understand the twitter of birds. They warn him of Regin, who is planning to poison the conquering hero. Thereupon Sigurd also kills the deceitful Regin, thus becoming the sole owner of the fateful treasure. Sigurd hides the treasure and sets out on his journey. Sigurd finds Brynhild, who has been condemned to a deep sleep by Odin, in the middle of a ring of raging fire. Only a fearless hero can ride through this sea of flames and save Brynhild (figure 34, right).

After swearing an oath of eternal loyalty, Sigurd leaves Brynhild and rides on until he meets Gjuki, king of the Franks. He becomes a blood-brother with Gjuki's sons Gunnar and Hoegni. Gunnar's sister Gudrun offers Sigurd a magic potion, which makes him forget Brynhild and marry her (figure 34, left).

Gunnar now wants Brynhild to become his wife and manages to achieve this with Sigurd's help. Brynhild, however, wants to have Sigurd's presumed unfaithfulness punished. Guttorm, Gunnar's youngest brother, kills Sigurd on Brynhild's request when stopping to rest at a spring. (figure 39)

Gudrun awaits the return of her husband from the hunt with fearful misgivings (figure 36).

After this crime, the murder of a blood-brother, has been committed, Brynhild mocks her husband Gunnar and lets him know that she never really loved him. Only Sigurd was the sole object of her love (figure 37).

While Gudrun mourns Sigurd's death (figure 40) a pyre of wood is being erected on which the hero is to be cremated. At the pyre Brynhild stabs herself and is cremated together with Sigurd (figure 40).

38.The Dragon: *"Regin hath betrayed me, he shall betray thee too!"*

39. Sigurd's death: *"South of the Rhine, Sigurd was killed."*

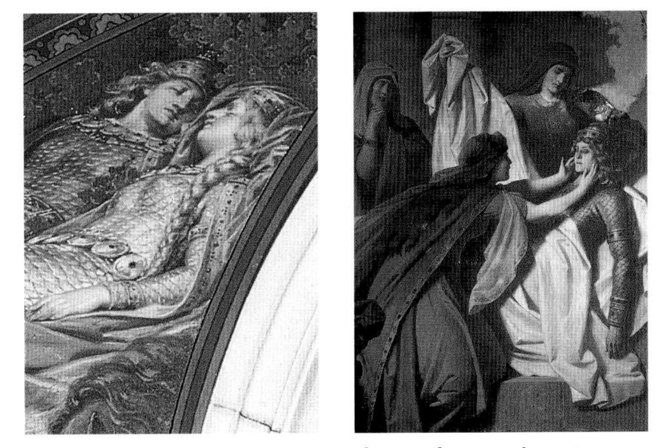

40. To the right of the door: Gudrun's lamentation: *"No tear could Gudrun shed, so great was her grief at her husband's death...".* ***Left: Brynhild is cremated together with Sigurd.***

The Throne Hall

The most splendid and impressive room in the Castle of Neuschwanstein is without a doubt the Throne Hall with its almost sacred atmosphere (figure 41). Unfortunately it has remained unfinished as the most important object of this room, the throne, is missing. After the unexpected death of the King his family canceled all the uncompleted contracts for orders already placed with suppliers so that work on the throne was never started. Sketches showing the plans for a magnificent throne give us an idea of what the King had in mind (figures 42 and 43).

It was in this Throne Hall that King Ludwig II wanted to pay homage to the idea of royalty as bestowed by the grace of God. The throne was to be placed on top of the marble stairs in the apse of the hall similar to an altar in a Byzantine church. The missing throne, more than anything else, points out the incongruity between Ludwig II's exalted ideal of a sacrosanct monarchy and the political facts of the time.

The paintings in the Throne Hall were painted by professor Wilhelm Hauchild. Six sanctified Kings standing between palm trees are depicted in the apse overlooking the space reserved for the throne (figure 41). From left to right: Kasimir

41.

of Poland, Stephen of Hungary, Henry II of Germany, Louis IX of France, Ferdinand of Spain and Edward the Confessor of England.

The apses of the All Saints Church (Allerheiligenhof), which was unfortunately destroyed during the War, the Karl's Church in Munich or the Strasbourg Cathedral all have a similar arrangement of sanctified kings. These churches probably inspired Ludwig II to have the Throne Hall designed in this manner.

The apse is crowned by Christ sitting on a rainbow. At his side are Mary, John and angels in prayer (figure 41).
To the left and to the right of the staircase the twelve apostles represent the Holy Laws of God (figure 44).

The other wall paintings in the apse illustrate excerpts from the lives of the sanctified kings. The barrel vaults supporting the dome depict pre-Christian legislators.
The illustrations in detail:
In the uppermost vault over the entrance: "The Roman Emperor Augustus", symbolizing 'Lex Romana' or Roman law. To his left Zarathustra, to his right Solon (figure 46).

42. Plan of a throne, Ed. Ille, 1876

43. Plan of a throne, Gg. v. Dollmann, 1879

44. The twelve apostles

45. The Old Testament
< 41. The Throne Hall with apse

46. Roman law

47. Lucifer's Fall

48. St. George's fight with the dragon

On the wall opposite the balcony one can see Moses with the Ten Commandments representing the Old Testament (figure 45). In the uppermost arch facing the apse the three Magi and their star symbolize the moral laws of Christianity as laid down in the New Testament (figure 55). Below that we can see Archangel Michael defeating Lucifer and Lucifer's descent into Hell (figure 47). Below that there is a painting especially worth mentioning: Saint George's fight with the dragon who symbolizes evil (figure 48). A castle resembling Neuschwanstein can be seen on top of a mountain at the left of the painting. It is actually a fourth castle which King Ludwig II planned to build on Falkenstein, a rocky peak near Pfronten in southern Bavaria, to replace the ruin of a castle already there. The plans for this castle were nearly completed, a road as well as water pipes leading to the building site were already finished. Here again the sudden death of the King stopped all further building projects.

To the left of the entrance: King Edward the Confessor of England as an impartial judge (figure 52). To the right of the entrance: King Ferdinand the Catholic of Spain fighting against the Moors to liberate Spain (figure 49). Above the entrance to the left: King Stephen of Hungary converting the Hungarians to Christianity. To the right: The German emperor Henry II at the building of Bamberg Cathedral.
On the opposite side, to the left of the door to the balcony: Saint Elizabeth showing mercy (figure 51). To the right: The canonized Queen Klothilde of France converts her husband to Christianity (figure 53).
To the right of the door: King Kasimir of Poland rapt in prayer (Figure 50). Directly above: King Louis IX of France feeds the poor (figure 54).

The Throne Hall is 15 meters (approx. 45 ft) high and 20 meters (approx. 60 ft) long. The mosaic floor, which depicts the terrestrial sphere with all the animals and plants, is a particularly fine piece of work (made by Detoma, Vienna, following the design of A. Spenger) (figure 55).

49. King Ferdinand the Catholic of Spain

50. Kasimir of Poland at prayer ***51. Saint Elizabeth***

52. Edward the Confessor

53. Klothilde of France converts her husband.

54. Louis IX of France feeds the poor

55.

The dome symbolizes the heavens with the sun and stars. The chandelier, shaped like a Byzantine crown, is made of gold plated brass, set with glass stones and imitation ivory. It holds 96 candles. The crown-shaped chandelier is meant to symbolize the position of the King as intermediary between heaven and earth. The heavy chandelier weighing approximately 900 kilograms (2000 pounds) hangs from an iron chain, that can be moved by means of a winch installed in the loft over the Hall. Thus it is possible to lower the chandelier to the floor in order to clean it and exchange the used candles. The King never saw this chandelier. It was not completed until after his death and was placed in the Throne Hall in 1904. The pillars in the lower part of the Throne Hall are made of purple colored stucco imitation porphyry, the ones in the upper part of stucco in the color of lapis lazuli.

On leaving the room one can see the vents of the central warm air heating system built somewhat above the floor to the right and left of the door. Five big heating stoves installed on the first floor served to moderately heat the main building of the castle complex. The rooms in the King's living quarters, however, had additional built in tiled stoves.

The View from the Balcony

From the balcony of the Throne Hall (not accessible for visitors) the King had a magnificent view of one of the most beautiful and charming countrysides in Bavaria. To the left, the crystal clear Lake Alpsee and to the right, the smaller Swan Lake (Schwansee). Between the two lakes, the ancient site of Hohenschwangau Castle (originally called 'Schwanstein') (figure 56). Commissioned by crown-prince Max (later King Max II), Hohenschwangau Castle as it is today was reconstructed between 1832 and 1838 by the Quaglio Brothers. It was there that Ludwig II spent most of his early years.

Rising behind the two lakes are the Tyrolian Alps (the Tannheimer Group). The border between Germany and Austria runs along the wooded hills behind Lake Alpsee.

Between Hohenschwangau Castle and Lake Alpsee, the ancient "Via Claudia", built by the Romans and a very important trade route in the Middle Ages, led from Augsburg to Rome. It continues from here, via Reutte in Tirol and the Fernpass, to Italy.

Just in front of the right shore of Lake Schwansee one can see the two quarries of Schwangau-Alterschrofen. The stones taken from here were used to cover the walls of Neuschwanstein Castle.

Leaving the Throne Hall and crossing the entrance hall one reaches a servant's room. Through an electrical calling system installed above the seat the valet was always within calling reach of the King. The seats are covered with pigskin.

56.

The Dining Room

The dining room (figure 57) is dominated by the massive centerpiece on the serving table, made of gold-plated bronze and manufactured by the Munich artisan Widmann following a design by Wollenweber (figure 66). The sculpture depicts Siegfried's fight with the dragon, which is a fight between good and evil - a motif frequently to be found in this castle (the fight with the dragon in the entrance hall to the third floor and St.George's victory over the dragon in the Throne Hall). The base of this centerpiece is made of polished Carrara marble. Two small cupboards for silverware which are richly decorated with woodcarvings are found to the right and left of the dining table. This room is also remarkable for its paneling which is decorated with highly ornate oak carvings. Curtains and draperies are made of dark red silk with splendid embroidery and appliqué work (these as well as all textile art in the King's quarters were manufactured by Joerres, Munich). The heavy candelabrum hanging from the ceiling is again made of gold-plated bronze, decorated with Bohemian stained glass (also from Wollenweber's studio). A stove in the Moorish style served as an extra heating device in addition to the already built-in central warm air heating system. The openings for the warm air system in all the rooms are concealed behind the wall paneling. There is no so-called 'ready-laid-table' ('Tischleindeckdich') in the castle of Neuschwanstein as there is in the castles of Linderhof and Herrenchiemsee.

57.

It was technically impossible to have such a table built in Neuschwanstein as the kitchen is situated three floors down. There was, however, a hand-driven food lift which made it possible for food to be served on all three floors of the castle.

58. The poems are returned to Heinrich von Veldecke

59. Klingsor at the court in Eisenach: *"Do come and buy, for here is a strange monster for sale, that no one hath ever laid eyes on and never more shall..."*

60. Count Hermann and Wolfram von Eschenbach

61. A recital by wandering minstrels

62. The Count entertains the singers

64. Klingsor's magic flight

63. Reiner von Zweter

65. The singers' competition at Wartburg Castle >

From the dining room window one has a fine view of the wildly romantic Poellat gorge with its 45 meter (approx. 150 ft.) waterfall. Queen Mary's Bridge ("Marienbruecke"), a bridge named after the King's mother Mary, spans the roaring mountain stream 91 meters (approx. 300 ft.) above the ground (figure 83). Beyond the bridge a winding path leads up to Mount Tegelberg. Replacing an old wooden footbridge, this bridge was built in 1866 as bridge number 146 by the firm Gerber, which later was to become the famous company MAN.

The paintings in the dining room depict scenes of life in Wartburg Castle at the time of the legendary singers' competition which is said to have taken place in 1207.
Prof. Ferdinand Piloty, a well-known painter from Munich, painted these pictures. The following scenes can be seen:

The recently stolen manuscript of the poem "Eneis" is returned to Heinrich von Veldecke through the mediation of Count Hermann (figure 58).

The magician Klingsor, who is to be the arbitrator of the singers' competition, arrives at the Court and says to the Count: "Do come and buy, for here is a strange monster for sale, that no one hath ever laid eyes on and never more shall." (figure 59)

Heinrich von Ofterdingen's quarrel with Wolfram von Eschenbach in the Singers' Hall of Wartburg Castle about which of the two gentlemen should receive the most praise, Count Hermann of Thuringia or Leopold, Duke of Hungary (figure 65).

Klingsor's magic flight with Heinrich von Ofterdingen to Wartburg Castle. It wasn't until the night before the festival that Klingsor summoned Heinrich to fly with him with the help of black magic from Hungary to Eisenach (figure 64).

The Count commissions Wolfram von Eschenbach to translate the poem "Willehalm" (figure 60).

A recital of the wandering minstrels in front of Wartburg Castle at the court of the Count of Thuringia (figure 61).

Count Hermann gives the wandering minstrels prizes and entertains them with great hospitality (figure 62).

66. Table centerpiece

Famous German minnesingers or minstrels are depicted over the three doors:
Over the door to the servants' room: Gottfried von Strasbourg, poet of the Middle High German version of "Tristan and Isolde" (figure 57).
Over the door with the red curtains: Wolfram von Eschenbach, dictating a poem to a scribe (figure 57).
Over the bedroom door: The minstrel Reinmar von Zweter (figure 63).

The Bedroom

Ludwig II had a particular fondness for elaborate bedrooms (figure 67). This bedroom has been designed in the late Gothic style. It is in this room that one finds the most intricate oak woodcarving, especially in the canopy over the bed, the dressing table, the reading chair and the center pillar (woodwork by the firm Poessenbacher and Ehrengut, Munich).

An allegorical representation of love ("Minne") can be found to the left of the dressing table and, to the right, a representation of faithfulness ("Triuwe").

The bed is very large because the king himself, a fine figure of a man, was 1.91 meters tall (approx. 6'4"). The head of the bed is embellished with a copy of an icon painted on a gilded copper plate by J. Frank (figure 68).

A relief carving of the resurrection of Christ, symbolic of the relationship between sleep and death is to be found at the end of the bed (figures 67 and 69).

The curtains and the furniture coverings (made by the firm Joerres in Munich) are in the King's favorite color, royal blue. The swan, the Bavarian coat of arms and the Wittelsbach lion have been chosen as motifs for the elaborate embroidery. During the king's lifetime, all of the

67.

windows and doors were draped with heavy curtains such as these. It has been necessary to remove most of the curtains to facilitate the tours through the castle.

The washstand is complete with running water. By turning the knob to the right under the table the user had running water coming from the silver swan. To empty the wash basin, it was simply tipped to the side and the water entered the castle's sewage system. To the left of the washstand, there is a secret door which is integrated into the wall paneling. This door leads to the King's toilet (not open for visitors). The cupboard to the right of the door to the dining room was used to store bed linen.

68. Madonna by J. Frank

69. Woodcarving on the bedstead

70. The washstand

To the right of the reading chair there is a large tiled stove designed in the Gothic manner. It is decorated with two clay figures, Tristan with his trusty sword and Isolde Blondhaar with a rose (figure 71).

A door to the left of the reading chair leads to a small balcony which offers a beautiful view of the Poellat Gorge and its waterfall. To the left there is a cozy corner seat in a bay window. The coats of arms of Schwangau, Wittelsbach and Bavaria can be seen in the painted glass windows (figure 73).

Over the door to the dining room there are three niches with the carved figures of Tristan, Isolde and King Marke (figure 72). In the arched segment over the door there is a painting of a lady in a local costume from the 15th century. She is holding a book of the 'Tristan' saga in her hands. In the background of the painting there is a scroll with the first verse of the poem. A rough translation into today's language would be. "It is told a story of love, a love sweet and always of new, of its devout faithfulness, and sorrow, its delight and its woe" (figure 72).

A free-standing Gothic wooden pillar in the middle of the room supports the heavy oak ceiling. Four minnesingers, also carved of oak, decorate the pointed arches at the top of the pillar.

It was here in this very room, on 12 June 1886, that the King was declared insane and legally incapacitated by a commission from Munich on the basis of a medical report. The King was taken to Castle Berg on Lake Starnberg on that very day where on the next day he died under extremely mysterious circumstances.

71. The reading chair and tiled stove in the bedroom

72. Woodcarving over the door with a painting of a medieval lady with a book

The wall paintings depict scenes from the saga of "Tristan and Isolde" which Richard Wagner immortalized in one of his operas. Here is a summary of this very long saga:

In the loneliness of a forest, desperate, abandoned by her husband, Elisabeth, the Queen of Leonois, gives birth to a baby boy. Elisabeth dies during the birth. Due to the sad events accompanying his birth, the boy is given the name Tristan (trist = sad). His father, King Meliadus, brother-in-law of King Marke of Cornwall, takes the child to have him raised and educated at his court.

When Tristan reaches adulthood he goes out into the world with his companion Kurwenal where he encounters many adventures. Finally, they come to Cornwall where King Marke recognizes his nephew and receives him as a son. On behalf of his patron, Tristan travels with Kurwenal to Ireland to ask for the hand of Isolde Blondhaar for the king. Tristan knows Isolde from the time when she healed his wounds with her magic potions. Tristan renders several very good deeds for King Hanguin of Ireland and thus is successful in winning over Isolde and can bring the beautiful bride home to King Marke. During their passage the wind stops and the ship floats helplessly on the calm sea. As the two travelers are very thirsty, Brangaene, Isolde's trusted companion, wishes to offer them both something refreshing to drink. Making a fatal mistake, she gives them the love potion which was intended for the aging King Marke.

73. The bay window in the bedroom

74. The offering of the love potion: *"...and both of them assumed that it was wine..."*

Tristan and Isolde, passionately in love, fall into each other's arms. After their arrival in Cornwall, Isolde is married to King Marke. Tristan, however, secretly meets Isolde again and again in the garden (figure 77). This affair between Tristan and the wife of the king is the cause of much gossip at the court. Marke, having become more and more suspicious, surprises the lovers in the garden (figure 75). Marke sentences Tristan to death at the stake, but with Kurwenal's help, Tristan is able to escape.

Outlawed and ill, Tristan finds refuge in Brittany with King Hoel and his daughter Isolde Weisshand where the daughter is able to restore Tristan's health with her magic potions. As a sign of gratitude for Tristan's heroic deeds, King Hoel gives Tristan the hand of his daughter. Tristan does not, however, share his wife's bed but rather abandons her and joins King Arthur's Round Table.

After many adventures, Tristan is able to render a great service to his uncle King Marke who then allows him to return to court. Jealous courtiers stir up hatred, turning the king against his nephew by convincing him that Isolde is still meeting secretly with Tristan. In anger Marke sneaks into the chamber where Tristan is singing a ballad to his mistress and stabs the singer in the side with a poisoned spear. Tristan, fatally wounded, has himself brought to the castle of his wife, Isolde Weisshand, so that she can again heal him with her magic potions. The jealous wife, however, refuses to help him. It is here that Tristan receives the news that King Marke has forgiven him and is coming to Tristan along with Isolde Blondhaar. Weaker and weaker, close to death, languishing, Tristan awaits Isolde. (figure 76).

Finally the ship brings Isolde, Marke and Kurwenal to Tristan's castle. With feigned sympathy, Marke asks his nephew for forgiveness. Tristan refuses and dies. Isolde Blondhaar breaks down at Tristan's death bed and dies (figure 78). And thus it is that the two lovers are finally joined together in death.

75. King Marke surprises Tristan and Isolde

76. Tristan on his sickbed

77. Tristan and Isolde in the garden in Cornwall: *"And so he and his beloved Isolde came to the fountain in the shade of an olive tree..."*

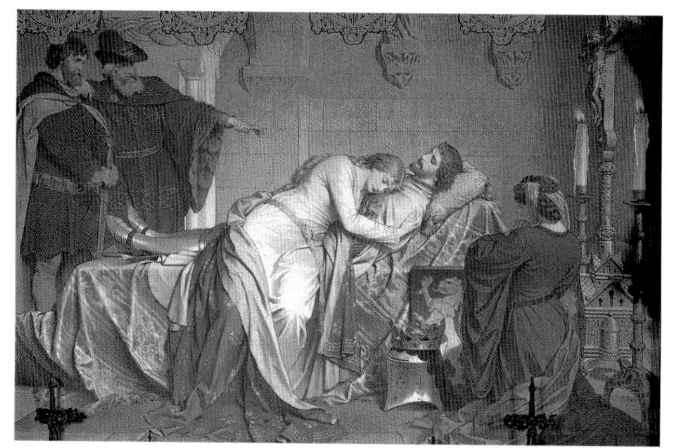

78. Isolde's love death ("Liebestod"): *"She held him tightly in her arms and kissed him tenderly on his lips and cheeks. And night befell her senses and without lament she pined away and died..."*

The Private Chapel

King Ludwig II, who was a deeply religious person, attached great importance to having a small room for prayer in each of his castles. The architect Julius Hofmann planned this chapel for Neuschwanstein in 1880 (figure 81). Two doors lead into the chapel, one from the bedroom and the other from the dressing room. The small room has a vault of pointed arches in the Gothic style with golden stars shining on a royal blue background in the ceiling panels. The painting at the altar shows the namesake of the king, King Louis (Ludwig) IX of France. In each of the side panels of the altar there is a painting of an angel. The backs of the side panels are decorated with carved grape vines and foliage. Underneath the small capitals to the left and right of the altar there are also busts of angels carved from oak.

The paintings (by W. Hauschild) show scenes from the life of Louis IX of France:

To the left of the altar: Saint Louis receives a crusade flag from a bishop (figure 79).

Over the door to the bedroom: The death of Louis IX during a crusade.

The painted glass in the window (by F. Mayer, Munich): Saint Louis receives the last rites (figure 81).

On the altar table, flanked by two candelabra, is a crucifix. The cross is of ebony while the body of Christ is carved from one piece of ivory, with the exception of the arms which were carved separately (A. Diesel, Munich 1883) (Figure 80).

79. Saint Ludwig receives the crusade flag

80. Ivory crucifix

81. The private chapel

In winter Castle Neuschwanstein looks like a fairy-tale cast-le (figure 82).

From the road to Bleckenau one has an especially beautiful view of the castle from under Queen Mary's Bridge (Marienbruecke) (figure 83).

82. The west facade of the castle

83. Queen Mary's Bridge (Marienbruecke) and castle

84.

Like an unset jewel, framed by the magnificent countryside, Neuschwanstein Castle stands high on the rocks and can be seen from afar (figures 84 and 85).

It was of the utmost importance to King Ludwig II that his castles were built in complete harmony with the surrounding countryside.

85.

The Dressing Room

The dressing room is the only room in the King's apartment which does not have a wooden ceiling. Instead there is a painting of an open arbor on the ceiling. All the paintings in this room are by Edward Ille, a pupil of Moritz von Schwind. They depict scenes from the life of Walther von der Vogelweide (1170-1230), a medieval minstrel, and from the lives of the Meistersingers of Nuremberg. The large washstand with its top of black marble is decorated with oak carvings. A costly set of washing utensils made by the well-known firm Villeroy and Boch from Mettlach in Saarland used to be on display here (figure 86). It was removed to be exhibited in the King Ludwig II Museum on the island of Herrenchiemsee when the museum was re-opened. The set to be seen here at Neuschwanstein is the less extravagant version which was to have been used on the third floor of the gate house. A tiled stove is facing the washstand. Furniture and wall paneling are carved from ivory (made by Poessenbacher and Ehrengut, Munich). The curtains and cushion covers in violet colored silk are embroidered with a peacock motif (figure 88).

86.

The King's jewelry case is located on a small table in the corner (figure 88). The precious miniature painting on the front of the case by Professor August Spiess is titled "The Right of the First Wedding Night" - 'Jus primae noctis'. It is based on a painting by Garnier. It was in this jewelry case that the King kept his jewelry. Whatever jewelry was left, after some of it having been sold upon the death of King Ludwig, is now on exhibit at the Royal Treasury in the Munich Residence of the King.
On the door to the living room there is a very beautiful door lock made of polished wrought iron from the work-shop of Karl Moradelli, Munich (figure 87).

An exceptionally high standard in the field of arts and crafts was reached in Bavaria during the construction of King Ludwig's castles. Thus, when restoring Bavarian monuments after World War II, it was possible to rely on a tradition of highly trained artisans thanks to the explicit encouragement of the arts and crafts by King Ludwig II.

87. Wrought iron door lock

88. Jewelry case. In the background: Curtain embroidered with a peacock motif

89. Walther summons to the crusade.

The pictures in the dressing room are as follows:

Over the door to the living room: Walther von der Vogelweide (famous medieval poet and minnesinger) as a young man at his father's court with his feathered friends (figure 86). To the right over the washstand: Walther sings a song in praise of German traditions at the court of Duke Welf VI (figure 86). Over the window: Walther, as an old man next to a stone cross, appeals to the German sovereigns to take part in a crusade (figure 89). To the left over the stove: Walther rides from castle to castle (figure 91).
In the center, over the tiled stove: Hans Sachs with his circle of friends Pirkheimer, Vischer, Duerer and others. In the background the Nuremberg Castle and the St. Lawrence Church (figure 91).
To the right: Walther sitting on a rock in front of Wartburg Castle. This is an illustration of one of his poems, "As I was sitting on a rock" (figure 91). Over the door to the bedroom: Walther with Frederick of Austria on a crusade (figure 90). Further to the right: An illustration of Walther's poem "Beneath the Linden Tree" (figure 86).
Over the window in the niche, not visible to visitors, there are three paintings from the life of Hans Sachs: Sachs hands over the master's necklace (Meisterkette) to a young singer, Sachs with his family, and Sachs in his study.
A small door leading to the private chapel can be found next to the tiled stove.

90. Walther with Frederick of Austria on a crusade: *"Now for the first time, can I live without sorrow, since with mine own eyes have I seen the Holy Land..."*

91. Walther rides from castle to castle ***The Meistersingers of Nuremberg*** *"As I was sitting on a stone..."*

According to the King's original plans, there was to be a tower, 90 meters (approx. 270 ft) high in the upper courtyard of the castle (figures 5, 22, 24 and 25). Such a tower was an absolute necessity for any fortified medieval castle.

After Ludwig's death, the construction of this tower was not carried out for financial reasons. It had also been planned to build a spacious chapel on the ground floor of the tower. In 1988, when the upper court of the castle was paved, the outline of the plan of the tower and the church which were never built were marked with white stone slabs (figure 92).

The entire facade of the castle of Neuschwanstein was covered with slabs of limestone. This material was won in Alterschrofen near Swan Lake (Swansee). The supporting walls were built of brick.

92. The upper courtyard of the castle

The Living Room

The interior decoration of this spacious hall, which was the King's living room, was designed by Julius Hofmann (figure 94). A small room is divided from the main parlor by a row of pillars. It was in this small area, the so-called 'swan's corner', that King Ludwig is said to have particularly liked to sit and read (figure 94). The floor of this reading corner is still covered with the original rugs. Machine- woven rugs such as this one used to be in all of the rooms of the King's living quarters. The large rugs themselves were made from separate wide rugs. In case of damage the smaller rugs

93.

94.

could thus easily be exchanged. The castle was used as a storage place for objects of art and paintings during World War II. During this time the rugs were removed and moved to an unknown place. Most of these rugs have never turned up again - they were probably destroyed during the war.

The four pillars that divide the swan's corner from the main part of the living room have richly carved capitals. They depict the bust of Christ, of an emperor, a king and a crusader. The sculptures are intended to symbolize the foundation of the medieval world in Germany Light blue silk curtains embroidered with swan motifs hang next to the pillars and at the windows. In the bay window there is a life-size swan of enameled and glazed pottery which was made by the famous porcelain manufacturer in Nymphenburg (figure 93). There is a covered opening in the swan's back. This was intended to serve as a vase for flowers.

The large chandelier is made out of gold-plated brass and is adorned with 48 candles. It is perhaps interesting to note that the number of candles in all of the large chandeliers in the castle can be divided by 12. The historical reason for this number is that, according to the "Revelation of St. John", the holy city of Jerusalem had twelve gates and for every one of those gates to the sacred city of light there is a candle.

95. Above the door to the grotto: Lohengrin leaves the Castle of the Holy Grail: *"Now bring back the horse to its manger! I shall travel on with this bird wherever he may go..."*

The paintings in the living room depict scenes from the Lohengrin saga. Here is a short summary of the saga which was the source of inspiration for one of Richard Wagner's operas.

Elsa, Duchess of Brabant, is accused of fratricide by Ortrud and Telramund. Although Elsa claims her innocence, the accusation is taken to the emperor who orders a trial by ordeal. A knight is to fight for Elsa against Telramund. If Elsa's warrior is victorious her innocence will be proved. Through the miracle of the Holy Grail , Lohengrin is designated to give her counsel (figure 95). Traveling with a swan's barque, Lohengrin departs from Montsalvat, the Castle of the Grail, to come to Elsa's assistance.
Before the assembled knights and an astonished crowd of people, the swan lands with Lohengrin in Antwerp (figures 96 and 98). After landing, the swan turns itself into an angel (figure 100). Elsa tells Lohengrin of her sufferings. She happily accepts Lohengrin's offer to fight for her at her trial by ordeal.

Lohengrin conquers Telramund in battle and thus proves Elsa's innocence (figure 100). Elsa marries Lohengrin. Lohengrin makes it clear to Elsa that she should never ask his name or of his origin. If she should do so despite his warning, he would have to leave her and return to his father.
After several years, during which time Elsa gives birth to two children by Lohengrin, Elsa is insidiously pressured by Ortrud on the way to the cathedral (illustration not visible to visitors as it is behind the bookshelf between the two windows). Elsa should give Ortrud precedence for she is more worthy as a wife than one who does not even know her husband's name. In desperation Elsa asks Lohengrin the fateful question (figure 94). With a saddened heart, Lohengrin takes leave of his wife and his children to return to the Castle of the Grail (figure 97).

96. Lohengrin is greeted by the emperor

97. Lohengrin's farewell : *"Now must I take my leave! And then came with great speed his friend, the swan, with a barque..."*

The furniture and the wall paneling as well as the heavy wooden ceiling all have very ornamental oak carving. The closed bookcase between the windows is a copy of a bookcase which is in Wartburg Castle in Eisenach (figure 99). The paintings on top of the doors to the bookcase by Ferdinand Piloty are painted on a gold background and depict the following themes:

Left: Gottfried von Strassburg with a lady and a monk who is holding a poem about Tristan in his hands.

Center: Wolfram von Eschenbach presents the poem of Parsifal to the Duke of Thuringia. Above, two angels with the Holy Grail.

Right: The blind poet of the Song of the Nibelungen with a monk and a bishop. Above, Krimhilden's dream of the two black eagles which strike a white falcon, an omen of Siegfried's death.

The coats of arms of the ancient lineage that have to do with the Lohengrin Saga, which is the leitmotif for this room, can be found on the ceiling.

99. Bookcase

The same question is often posed by visitors to the castle who would like to know why it was that King Ludwig II had his residential quarters built on the 4th floor. It would have been so much more convenient to have had the King's apartments on the 2nd floor rather than having the servants' quarters put in there. The answer to this question is actually quite simple. In medieval times every castle lord had his residence as high as possible within the castle for the simple reason that, because of the limited range of the weapons, a siege and attack would have destroyed the lower floors first. It was King Ludwig's wish to build a castle like the ones from the Middle Ages and it is for this reason that he choose the same layout of the rooms.

One could speak of an anachronism, for the King preferred a medieval style on the one side, while at the same time made use of the most modern technical achievements of his time. Here is a very interesting statement by the King's counselor Duefflipp answering on behalf of the monarch to a similar question: "Why should one do without such modern things, which one surely would have made use of in the Middle Ages had they been known."

The upper court of the Castle is surrounded by three buildings:
On the side facing the gorge there is the so-called "Kemenate", a building which in the Middle Ages served as a residence for the ladies of the castle.

The original foundations for this building were leveled after the death of the King. In 1890 Prince Regent Luitpold had the "Kemenate" built in a simpler form. The interior, however, has never been completed.

To the west the upper courtyard is enclosed by the castle itself where one finds the private residence of the King and the state rooms.

On the east facade, directly under the gable, there are two paintings:
Left: "St. George in battle with the dragon"
Right: "The Patron Saint of Bavaria"

The long building on the north side of the court is the Knights' Hall (Ritterbau) also called Duerrnitz (figure 92).

100. The swan's corner in the living room

101.

The Grotto and the Winter Garden

In accordance with the romantic tastes of his time, Ludwig II had an artificial cave with stalactites built between the living room and the study (figure 101). Effectively lit through niches in the rocks and complete with a waterfall (no longer running) the cave was also connected to the warm air central heating system. The well known landscape sculptor from Munich, August Dirrigl, who also built the grotto in the park of Linderhof Castle, built this extremely realistic cave using broken flax and plaster-of-Paris over a steel frame. The cave was intended to represent the cave in Mount Hoesel from the Tannhaeuser saga.

Leaving the grotto, to the right after the living room, one reaches the entrance to the winter garden (figure 192). The glass door with an etched swan is made from a single piece of glass and can be completely sunk into the rock off to the left. The fountain in the winter garden was originally intended to decorate a hall in the Moorish style on the 3rd floor. As the work on the 3rd floor was never completed, the fountain, which had already been delivered, was placed in the winter garden. Through the window of the winter garden one has an especially beautiful view of Lake Forggensee.

102.

The King's Study

The King's study is similar to the study in the Wartburg Castle which was a model for the castle of Neuschwanstein. The room is built in the Romanesque style. Covered by a beautiful oak ceiling, the heavy curtains and furniture coverings of green silk are particularly worthy of notice. They are embroidered with the Bavarian coat of arms and were made by the firm Joerres in Munich. The elaborate oak woodcarvings were made by the firm Poessenbacher and Ehrengut in Munich.

The ornate pieces of wrought iron were made by the firm Moradelli in Munich. The firm Wollenweber in Munich made the candelabra and the writing utensils for the desk. To the right there is an oak bookcase in which the King is said to have stored his plans and rough drafts for his building projects. Opposite the bookcase there is a small tiled oven made of earthenware. The large desk used to be directly in front of the window and there was also another table in the room. To make room for the many visitors, furniture and curtains were removed from the study, as well

as from other rooms. These objects are stored in the castle in an extensive storage room where they are well protected and preserved. Also many personal things, which belonged to the King and which would be in great danger of being stolen, are kept in storage to be preserved for art historians and future generations.

Most of the paintings in the castle have as a motif themes upon which Richard Wagner based his operas. Here in the King's study it is the saga of the Knight of Tannhaeuser who is said to have lived for a year with Venus, the goddess of love, in a grotto. Richard Wagner combined this story with the story of "The Singers' Contest" to create one of his most famous operas (Tannhaeuser).

The painter Joseph Aigner from Munich painted this theme on large canvases so that the paintings have the appearance of Gobelins. According to legend, the painter worked too slowly for the king and hence was replaced by another painter in order that the paintings might be completed sooner. This interference with his artistic endeavors is said to have driven Aigner insane.

Here's a summary of the medieval saga of "Tannhaeuser":

A shepherd boy is playing a song on his shawm, a song of Venus, the Goddess of Love (figure 109). The song tells the story of how Tannhaeuser was lured by Venus into the magic mountain (Mount Hoersel near Eisenach) where she resided in a fantastic grotto (figure 106).

After some time the knight leaves the mountain of Venus to live again among people. As he is leaving Mount Hoersel he meets Count Herman in front of Wartburg Castle (figure 104). Together with other knights and minstrels Tannhaeuser rides into Wartburg Castle (figure 105).

104. Tannhaeuser meets the Count of Thuringia.

105. The singers ride into Wartburg Castle. *"One crowd goes, the next one comes, and so it goes day and night..."*

106. Tannhaeuser with Venus in Mount Hoersel: *"There was he again inside the mountain, and therein he now must stay..."*

107. The singers' competition: *"The count is in such high spirits, that he squanders all his belongings with valiant knights..."*

During the singers' competition, Tannhaeuser becomes so carried away that he sings a song of praise to the Goddess of love, thereby greatly angering the court and the knights (figure 107).

As penance he must make a pilgrimage to the Pope in Rome to ask for forgiveness for his sins. Urban IV refuses to give absolution to the penitent Tannhaeuser, who is begging for redemption. Urban says to Tannhaeuser: "Only when the thin staff in my hand begins to grow fresh foliage, will God forgive you (figure 110).

Contrary to the severeness of the Pope, God grants the penitent a sign of forgiveness - the Pope's staff actually does sprout leaves the very next day - but it is too late: Tannhaeuser is in such a state of despair after hearing the words of the Head of the Church that he returns to the Mountain of Venus. The medieval poem ends with the following verse:

> *This should a priest never more do*
> *Deny his people consolation -*
> *And if a man does penance and feels remorse*
> *His sins shall be forgiven!*

108. Lohengrin, the Knight of the Swans, crowns the King's writing utensils.

109. A shepherd boy plays on his shawm.

110. Tannhaeuser as penitent before the Pope: *"Oh, Pope, my dear Father! I confess my sins..."*

111. Tannhaeuser plays music for a circle dance: *"Sad hearts will be happy again, his merry song calls the damsels to dance..."*

The Adjutant's Chamber

The King's personal adjutant was accommodated in this room. In the left corner there is a bench which served as a chest for storage. During the day it was a place to sit; at night it could be converted into a bed. An electrical staff locator is installed behind the tiled stove to the right. The King was able to call his adjutant from every room of his residence. First a bell rang and then an optical signal indicated from which room the call came. The call system was run with a dry battery.

The curtains and coverings in this room are made from blue wool into which gold thread has been woven. Such curtains were hung from all of the windows and doors as well as between the pillars. Today most of these valuable pieces are in storage. The furniture, the wooden ceiling and wooden paneling are, as in all the other rooms, made of oak. The beautiful door locks of polished wrought iron are well worth noting.

The room for the valet de chambre is entered through a door in the back of the adjutant's chamber. In this room there is also a 'fold-up bed' and an electrical calling system similar to that in the adjutant's chamber.

On the north side, between the two windows, just under the ceiling, the so-called "Nuremberger Haeuschen" (Little Nuremberg House) can be seen. This little wall cupboard, for which the adjutant was personally responsible, was used as the King's medicine chest (figure 112).

112. The Little Nuremberg House ("Nuernberger Haeuschen")

113. The Adjutant's Room

114. The castle with Mount Saeuling at 2045 m (approx. 6,500 ft) in the background.

The Top of the Stairway

The center pillar of the main staircase, the staircase being reserved exclusively for the King when he was in residence, ends in a date palm of marble which seems to grow into heaven. Next to the pillar is a stone dragon which symbolically guards the tower. In the tower over the date palm, a small spiral staircase leads up to the top of the north tower which is 68 meters (approx. 223 ft) high (not open for visitors).

The Entrance Hall to the 5th floor

The entrance hall to the fifth floor is entered through a double glass door which is decorated with paintings in the upper part of the door. Two additional doors framed with marble lead from the hall, the one to the left leading to the gallery of the Singers' Hall and the one to the right leading to the gallery of the Throne Hall which is not open to the public. It is also in this entrance hall that one finds the small oak doors behind which are the servants' stairs.

The wall paintings by Wilhelm Hauschild depict the second half of the Sigurd saga. The first part of the saga is illustrated in the entrance hall of the 4th floor.

After Sigurd's death Gudrun moves with her entourage to her sister Thora (figure 116). There, in loneliness, she hopes to forget her sorrows. She embroiders a tapestry depicting the heroic deeds of her ancestors (figure 118).

Atli, the King of the Huns and two other princes ask for Gudrun's hand (figure 119). Gudrun's mother urges her to accept Atli's proposal. He is, however, mainly interested in

116. Gudrun's journey to Thora: *"Seven times half a year was I with Thora, Hakon's maiden in Denmark..."*

117. Entrance hall to the fifth floor

the treasure of the Nibelung which is in Gudrun's possession. Finally, Gudrun accepts Atli's offer and sets off in a bridal procession to the court of the King of the Huns.

After having lived for several years with Atli and having given him a son, Gudrun wishes to satisfy her desire for revenge. She invites her brothers, who were responsible for Sigurd's death, to Atli's court. A messenger of Atli brings the fateful invitation to Gunnar's court (figure 120).

Gudrun greets Gunnar and Hoegni in the banquet hall at Atli's court (figure 122). Because of Atli's avarice with regard to the treasure of the Nibelung, there is a fight between the Huns and the Franconian knights which the Franks lose. Gudrun kills her child from Atli, cooks the child and serves it to her husband and his warriors (figure 117).

The following night she stabs Atli and goes to her brother Gunnar who is shackled in the Snake's Tower and is playing sad songs on a harp with his feet (figure 124).

118. Gudrun embroidering: *"For diversion she embroidered in gold, Danish Vikings in German halls...".*

119. The sovereign princes court Gudrun: *"Marry the prince, for if thou dost not, thou shalt live alone until thou art fettered by old age..."*

120. Atli's messenger: *"...a message he sent out to Gunnar through a knight of great wisdom, called Knefroed..."*

121. Left: Atli's dream: *"I thought, daughter of Gjuki, thou wast about to pierce my breast with a bared dagger..."*

Right: Gudrun's bridal procession with Atli: *"Seven days we rode across a cold land..."*

Gudrun also kills her brother who is the last Franconian survivor and then throws a torch into the castle (center, figure 117).

Subsequently, she tries to commit suicide by throwing herself into the sea. Instead of drowning she is carried by the waves to the opposite shore to the castle of King Jonakur who takes her as his wife. There she lives with him for many years as his queen (figure 117).

122. Gudrun receives her brother at Atli's court: *"Better would it be for thee, brother, to ride in armor, than to live at Atli's court with helmets decked with rings..."*

123. The battle between the Huns and the Franks: *"They captured Gunnar, friend of Burgundy, and began to gag and fetter him..."*

124. Gunnar in the Snake Tower: *"Gunnar took up the harp and played it with his feet and so could he play that all of the women wept..."*

125. The Gallery to the Singers' Hall

The entrance to the Singers' Hall leads through a gallery from which one has a beautiful view of Lake Forggensee, the town of Schwangau and the countryside around the city of Fuessen. Many paintings by F. Piloty and A. Spiess illustrating the saga of Parsifal decorate the Singers' Hall and the gallery.

The Paintings in the Gallery:

Parsifal meets a knight's family on a crusade on Good Friday. It was the King's wish that this painting be unveiled on Good Friday 1884. The painter , A. Spiess was reproached by the King because of the incorrect representation of the horse. Ludwig, being a great horse enthusiast, saw immediately that it is impossible for a horse to stand on two legs! A horse must always have at least three legs on the ground when standing. The King, however, let it be and did not demand that the painting be changed as he had sometimes demanded with other paintings in the castle.

Gahmuret's arrival in Patelamunt, city of the Moors (figure 129). Gahmuret, second son of King Gaudin of Anjou, with a large entourage, enters the city belonging to Belakane, Princess of the Moors. The Princess has been wrongly accused of murdering King Eisenhart. Gahmuret conquers Belakanen's enemies in a tournament and marries the Moorish Princess (figure 131).
His son Feirefiz is conceived, but Gahmuret soon abandons Balakane and goes to France. During the journey he meets Queen Herzeloide who has proclaimed that a tournament will be held, the prize for the winner being the crown and her hand in marriage. Gahmuret is victorious and marries Herzeloide (figure 128). She is Parsifal's future mother.
Gawan, the nephew of King Arthur and the most shining of the Knights of the Round Table, brings about a reconciliation between Melianz and Obie, daughter of Lippaot, Duke of Beaurocher, which results in their engagement and marriage (figure 130). Later Gawan finds a badly wounded knight, cleanses and dresses his wounds and gives him medicinal herbs (figure 133).
Following an order by Kundries, Gawan frees queens and women held captive by Klingsor at Chatell Merveille Castle. It is in this magic castle that he survives various dangerous misadventures the last one being a fight with a lion. He is able to kill the lion but he is poisoned by the animal's breath and falls unconscious to the floor (figure 134).

126. Parsival meets a knight's family on Good Friday

127. Gawan in King Gramoflanz's garden

128. Gamuret marries Herzeloide

129. Gamuret's arrival in Patelamunt

130.Gawan reconciles Melianz and Obie

Queen Arnive and her ladies-in-waiting find Gawan and they are able to bring him back to life.
Gawan agrees to attempt at Orgeluse's behest, whom he later marries, a challenging heroic deed, that is, to take a branch from the tree in the garden of King Gramoflanz (figure 127). After Gawan has broken Klingsor's magic spell and freed the women in Chatell Merveille, he celebrates his marriage with Orgeluse (figure 132).

The names of famous minnesingers are engraved in the wooden ceiling of the gallery. The six chandeliers are made of gold-plated brass and decorated with colored glass (made by E. Wollenweber, Munich) (figure 125).

131. Gamuret at a tournament

132. Gawan marries Orgeluse

133. Gawan saves a wounded knight

134. Gawan's fight with the lion

135. Temperance

The Singers' Hall

After having visited Wartburg Castle in 1867, Ludwig II wished to build a replica of its banquet hall for himself. In 1868, when the Castle of Neuschwanstein was in the planning stage, one of the most important rooms in this new castle was to be the Singers' Hall (figure 136). King Ludwig II was deeply impressed by Richard Wagner's compositions. It was for this reason that he wanted to create in this room a realistic setting for the ideas and impressions that Wagner's compositions had kindled in his mind.

The architect Julius Hofmann designed the Singers' Hall in Neuschwanstein using both the banquet hall and the singers' hall of Wartburg Castle as his source of inspiration. According to the King's wishes, the furnishings of the hall were laid out even more sumptuously than those at Wartburg Castle.

The paintings in the Singers' Hall, beginning on the window side of the room from left to right, illustrate the Parsifal saga:
Parsifal hears about knighthood from Count Karnachkananz and how one can become a knight oneself (figure 138).

136.

Parsifal takes leave of his mother Herzeloide. She, however, dresses him in a jester's garb in the hope that he can be persuaded to return home sooner (figure 139).
Parsifal arrives at the court of King Arthur. Following the King's advice, Parsifal takes up battle with the Red Knight Ither. He conquers the knight and takes from him his horse and his armor (figure 137).
Parsifal comes to the aid of Queen Condviramour who is being plagued by her enemies. Parsifal conquers her enemies and marries the Queen (figure 140).
Soon tired of having nothing to do, Parsifal goes out into the world again. After a long journey he meets King Amfortas fishing in a lake. The king is ill. Amfortas invites Parsifal to

137. Parsifal's fight with the 'Red Knight'

138. Parsifal's first contact with the knights

visit Montsalvat, the Castle of the Holy Grail, where he will be hospitably received (figure 141).
Parsifal, warmly welcomed at the Castle of the Grail, takes part in a banquet for the Knights of the Grail. During the banquet, Amfortas, King of the Grail, who is greatly suffering from a spear wound, is carried into the banquet hall along with the poisoned spear. Foolishly, Parsifal does not have the courage to ask the expected question concerning the reason for the King's illness. It is only by asking this question that the King can be freed from his suffering (figure 148).

On the wall facing the courtyard, above in the two triangular spaces:
After the banquet, Parsifal is lead into a magnificent bedchamber where he is waited on by virgins. Parsifal is haunted until dawn by nightmares. Parsifal leaves the Castle of the Grail and is ridiculed by the guards for his foolishness (figure 149).

On the gallery wall from left to right:

Kundrie, the Messenger of the Grail, abuses and curses Parsifal because he has failed to ask the longed-for question (figure 143).
On Good Friday Parsifal comes to the hideaway where Trevrezent, the brother of Amfortas, lives as a hermit. The hermit takes Parsifal in and explains the secret of the Holy Grail to him (figure 144).
Parsifal meets his step-brother Feirefiz (figure 145).

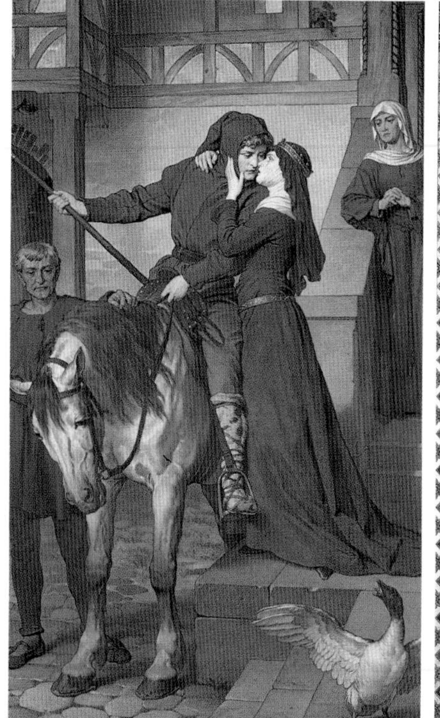

139. Parsifal's takes leave of his mother

140. Parsifal marries Condviramour

141. Parsifal's encounter with Amfortas

Parsifal finally asks Amfortas the question about the reason for his illness and is summoned a call to be King of the Grail by Kundrie (figure 142).
Parsifal hands over the rule of his inherited lands to his youngest son Kardeiz and assumes sovereignty as guardian of the Holy Grail. His brother Feirefiz marries Repanse, Amfortas's sister, and moves with her to India. Johannes, the priestly king, is their son.

On the wall over the singers' arbor at the top in the two spandels:
Left: Lohengrin, Parsifal's son, leaves the Castle of the Grail with a swan ship on his way to Elsa von Brabant.
Right: Repanse with the Holy Grail.

The large backdrop in the singers' arbor depicts Klingsor's magic garden (figure 152).

To the left and right of the backdrop, between climbing roses, paintings of minnesingers and allegories.

The immense ceiling of the room is made of pine wood. It is divided into coffers which are alternately decorated with ornaments and signs of the zodiac. Over the gallery hall there is a balcony with a ledge which is carried by two sculptured figures. To the left is Kyot (figure 146), writer and poet who found the discarded original version of the story of the Grail in Toledo, Spain and translated it. To the right is Flayetanis who read about the Holy Grail in the stars and then wrote the story (figure 147).

142. Kundrie summons Parsifal to the King of the Grail

143. Kundrie puts a curse on Parsifal **144. Parsifal with Trevrezent** **145. Parsifal encounters Feirefiz**

146.

A row of sculptured figures can be seen on the window side of the hall under the ceiling. From right to left: An anchor, the coat of arms of the Gahmurets.
A snake symbolizing the demonic forces working against the Holy Grail.
Satan's Fall during which a precious stone fell out of his crown. It was from this stone that the Holy Grail was cut (figure 151).
An angel, suspended in midair, holds this gem awaiting the Incarnation of Christ.
A griffin and a dragon which, as symbolic animals and as figures in coats-of-arms, often appear in the Parsifal saga.
A knight with the broken lance which was the cause of King Amfortas's infirmity.
A Knight of the Grail holding a shield and a spear.
The aloe tree whose wood was burned at the Castle of the Grail as a cure for Amfortas's suffering.
The pelican whose blood was also used to ease Amfortas of his pain.
The unicorn whose heart was to heal Amfortas's illness.
Klingsor the deceitful magician from the Orient who took the holy spear from Parsifal.

Below these figures there are many coats-of-arms and portraits painted on a gold background all having to do with the Parsifal saga.

147

148. Parsifal in Montsalvat, the castle of the Holy Grail

149. Parsifal is ridiculed

Allegories depicting knightly virtues of "strength, faithfulness, justice, steadfastness, temperance, blessedness, truth and wisdom" are distributed throughout the entire hall (figure 135).

The hall is lit with four enormous chandeliers and ten large candelabras, all made of gold-plated brass and decorated with Bohemian glass (by Wollenweber, Munich).

The King was never able to enjoy a concert in this hall. It wasn't until 1933, to commemorate the 50th anniversary of Richard Wagner's death, that the first concert was held and up to the beginning of the War in 1939, Wagner festival concerts took place here. A plaque in the lower courtyard still commemorates the famous musicians who took part. In 1952 the concert program was started again but due to a lack of funds these concerts were not successful and were soon discontinued.

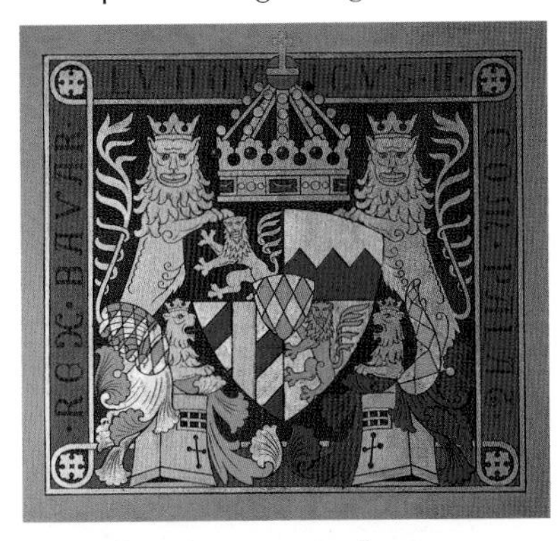

150. The King's coat of arms

At the 100th anniversary of the laying of the foundation stone in 1969 the economic situation in the country had improved to the point where it was once again possible to take up the concert series. Ever since then concerts, which are known way beyond the borders of Bavaria, have been held yearly in the castle. (Information about these concerts can be obtained at the Tourist Information Center, Schwangau.)

The coat-of-arms of the Bavarian king is depicted above the two small doors next to the singers' arbor (figure 150).

On the green borders around the coat-of-arms the following words are written in Latin: "Ludwig II., King of Bavaria, Count Palatine." This inscription is the only reference in the entire castle to its builder (the bust in the entrance to the "Red Corridor" was only placed there in 1988).

151. Lucifer's Fall

152. Klingsor's magic garden

The Kitchen

The kitchen in Neuschwanstein is, in contrast to the kitchens in the castles of Linderhof and Herrenchiemsee, still fully intact. The kitchen is in a large hall with a vaulted ceiling supported by two massive pillars (figure 153).

A large free-standing stove is to be found in the center of the kitchen. Behind the stove there is a kitchen counter and two blocks of maple wood for cutting meat. The kitchen was extremely modern for its time with running hot and cold water as well as fully automatic roasting spits. The roasting spits functioned in the following manner: The rising hot air in the chimney turned a turbine which in turn moved the gears to rotate the roasting spit. A charcoal grill was built next to the large roasting spit. To the right there is a cupboard for keeping the dishes warm. The smoke and the hot air from the large stove was directed to the left side of this cupboard and then to the chimney through a large underground pipe.

A small wood-burning oven for baking can be found in the right corner and next to it there is another small stove with a small roasting spit.

A built-in basin for fish can be seen under the window to the left of the balcony door. It has a faucet in the form of a swan's head. (The fixtures in this kitchen were delivered and built in by the firm 'Gas- und Wasserleitungsgesellschaft Stuttgart/Bad Canstatt.')

Kitchen counters were placed along the wall, one of these even had an 'ice-box'. Iron racks were hung over the counters for the copper pots and pans. The original kitchen utensils no longer exist. Today several pieces from other kitchens are on display. The kitchen was in use from 1884 to 1886. Although the King was only in the castle for 172 days during this time,it was still necessary to take care of the household staff.

153.

Between 10 and 15 persons were always present to maintain the building and the rooms. When the King was in residence the number of people on the staff was more than double that.

The balcony of the kitchen offers a beautiful view of the romantic Poellat Gorge with its waterfall and Queen Mary's Bridge (Marienbruecke) (figure 155).

Leaving the kitchen one comes into an antechamber which was the office for the chef du cuisine. It contains a large built-in cupboard for the tableware. From this room one can have a look at the scullery which is also still completely intact (figure 154).

154. The scullery

155. Queen Mary's Bridge (Marienbruecke) with Mount Saeuling

The large stoves for the hot air central heating system were located on the first floor. These rooms are not, however, open to visitors. The warm air from five stoves was directed through a system of pipes and shafts to the upper floors of the castle. A special elevator was installed to transport the enormous amount of firewood that was necessary for the kitchen and for the central heating.

156. King Ludwig II on the balcony of the Throne Room of the Castle of Neuschwanstein
(Painting by Ferdinand Leeke)

157. The Castle of Hohenschwangau, *rebuilt from 1832 to 1838 by Crown Prince Max of Bavaria, the father of Ludwig II, who later became King Maximilian II of Bavaria. The Crown Prince hired the brothers Quaglio to be the architects.*

158. Linderhof Castle *in the valley of Graswang (Graswangtal) near Oberammergau. This small rococo castle is the only one of all the King's castles on which construction work was completed.*

159. The Castle of Herrenchiemsee. *Ludwig II had this magnificent castle modeled after Versailles. The work on Herrenchiemsee was, however, only partially completed.*

160. *An interesting exhibition of the history of King Ludwig II and other Bavarian kings from the family of the Wittelsbacher is on permanet display at* ***the Royal Museum in Hohnschwangau.***